REPURPOSE YOUR CAREER

A PRACTICAL GUIDE FOR BABY BOOMERS

Marc Miller with Susan Lahey

Repurpose Your Career

Copyright © 2013 by Marc Miller

Career Pivot Publishing

ISBN 978-0-9887005-0-5

PRAISE FOR REPURPOSE YOUR CAREER

I love this book! It is highly readable, insightful and action-oriented. The concept of Career Pivots as a series of half-steps towards a goal brilliantly captures the process of career change.

Arlene S. Hirsch M.A., LCPC Career and Psychological Counseling, Chicago

If you're deciding what to do for Act Two of your career, read this book. Marc Miller's empathic, constructive suggestions will help you gain clarity to identify what direction to take, and his practical tips will help you successfully reach your goals.

Miriam Salpeter, Author *Social Networking for Career Success* and *100 Conversations for Career Success*, social media and job search consultant, www.KeppieCareers.com

Marc Miller talks about the elephant in the room that many baby boomers are avoiding... we are living longer and will have to work longer. But what does reinventing your career mean when you are in your 50s or 60s? You can repurpose your career and this book will help you tackle the changes and help you find fulfillment in your work and personal life.

Thom Singer, Author *The ABC's of Networking.*

Kudos to Marc for staying true to his goal of creating "A Practical Guide" for Baby Boomers as they tentatively navigate their way toward an often scary search for a new career.

His book has a laser focus on the key aspects to successfully accomplishing a midlife career change: Who am I? What do I really want to do? What matters to me in all aspects of my work? How to search for and land a job that will satisfy my needs? Midlife career transition is definitely not for sissies and Marc gives practical action steps along the path to success.

Laura Schlafly, Career Coach, Speaker, Author, *Creative Catalyst for Career Change.* Helping mid-life professionals find meaningful work with Passion, Purpose and a Paycheck. www.CareerChoicesWithLaura.com.

Marc has written a book those in career transition need to read. He stated he likes systems and that is exactly what he has provided—an organized approach to helping one find the position that doesn't seem like a job. Follow his system and you'll be well on your way to be able to laser focus your job search. People will understand what you are looking for and you will know how and with whom you should network to find the position that matches your personality and skills.

Kathy Condon, award-winning Author, Trainer and Speaker on Face-to-Face Networking

A sobering, inspiring and practical read for all. This book is not only for boomers; because all careers will pivot and we need to be ready for inevitable changes.

Gudjon Bergmann Author, Speaker and Writing Consultant www.authorsblueprint.com

This book is dedicated to my wife, Lotus, who has put up with me for 31 years. To my son, Alex, who has been a great teacher for me.

And to Jack, my cat.

ACKNOWLEDGMENTS

The genesis for this book began with my first career decisions in the 1970's. Over the years, I wandered around a lot in my career and therefore, I have lots of people to thank.

The first is my wife Lotus who has stood by me for over 30 years through my many trials and tribulations. Twice I recovered from major injuries where I spent months in bed and in rehabilitation, and she cared for me.

My son, Alex allowed me to understand myself through him. I have often told people that your children can be your greatest teacher. I am very proud of my son and the individual he has become.

My chiropractor, Michelle Girard, has stood by me and cared for me through my many injuries.

When I left corporate America to start Career Pivot, I could not have done it without Sherry Lowry. Sherry has been there every time I get down and discouraged. Sherry guided me to people who could form my team.

I want to thank Ginny Murphy who worked with me on my Career Pivot brand development.

Gudjon Bergmann, an author who has published many books of his own, has been a fountain of information throughout the process, I'm very grateful to him.

Lastly, my co-author, Susan Lahey, on this endeavor has been a real joy to work with. Susan has taken my thoughts and beautifully crafted them. I believe that writing this book has been a journey for her as well. A journey that I hope many of you will take to a better place.

FOREWORD BY SHERRY LOWRY

If living your life on purpose includes cultivating and enjoying a meaningful career, this book is for you. If you are on a career quest, these contents contain your map for a journey you will never regret undertaking.

Becoming your own Decider is the message. One of Marc's early decisions was to ask Susan Lahey to participate in helping him document his discoveries and processes as he took new career risks. He also developed his own support team, here in Austin and beyond.

 Prior to all this, he had a very close brush with death that changed his role in his own life. He became his own Decider. He committed to a series of career pivots that required significant personal change.

This book documents what Marc learned and shares with clients. If you want to bypass or recover from your own career-crash, or avoid waiting for another personalized, scary life experience as your wake-up call, you will find companionship for your own journey of discovery in the pages that follow.

Marc's Career Pivot approach can keep you realistic, yet safe, designing then acting upon half steps that will get you ultimately to your main goal. He gives a strategy, a logical plan, awareness of challenges ahead, and a set of tools to address these.

One immediate payoff is how clearly you will be able to actually name what it is you need to eliminate, add or move directly toward. Things you've known you've wanted but could not really describe or ask for concretely. Now you'll be able to do that both within your career environment as well as your personal relationships. Really. Like what?

How about being able to actually gain through really simple, small changes more of what you need in: flexibility, scheduling, organizational system, structure, respect, emotional support, more variety or more balance, interruption elimination, rewards, being accurately heard?

"What Do I Want" is one of life's most challenging inquiries. Marc's approach helps you answer it by identifying what you DON'T want.

I know by now some of you must be wondering where and how passion comes into all this. If you've discovered yours but don't quite know how to pursue it, there is help ahead. First though, a passion has many avenues of expression. They don't ALL get fulfilled in any one location — so yours may find its best home in an area fueled by your career, though possibly not directly within it.

This book also gives special emphasis to the significance of relationships — well beyond the ordinary clichés you've heard and discarded around "networking." For a purposeful refashioning or design of a gratifying career, building new and even healthier existing relationships is a sacred undertaking. This book has heart around this process.

You've made a good choice. This book is partially research-based, it is incredibly practical, and it has heart. You will find you can return to it repeatedly — including during and following each stage of your own half steps toward your most wanted changes. It is a book that becomes wiser and more meaningful each time you try out the concepts presented, then revisit it with what you learn and discover anew yourself.

There is an applicable, fundamental truth within about leadership: leading self is your most important life-skill. You are your own legacy. This can offer one source of support for you to become your own more conscious life and career architect.

That's now an essential part of the future for each of us: it's not only really what or who we know, it's what we continue to learn, the creativity we apply and the value we then share with others. These are our new currencies: our willingness to embrace change, to keep learning, and enrich our communities as well as ourselves with the results. Repurpose Your Career is a good primer in each.

I am grateful to Marc and Susan for sharing their talents and experiences on their own career repurposing journeys. I believe you will be also.

Sherry Lowry, Professional Mentor,
Business, Alliance and Collaboration Coach

TABLE OF CONTENTS

YOUR FIRST STEPS TOWARD YOUR NEW LIFE

I was on my way to China, literally standing in line waiting to board the plane, when the question that had been picking at the back of my mind sprung up in front of me, huge and fully formed: What are you DOING?

Less than a year before, I had survived a nearly fatal bicycle accident. My bike hit the car—head on—at combined speeds of 50 miles an hour. The car was totaled and so should I have been. But miraculously, though I spent five days in a trauma center, I recovered fully. At those speeds there is a 10 percent chance of survival.

I was alive. The one life I get, that I know of. And I was once again getting on a plane to go somewhere I didn't care to go to teach people how to design leading edge routers and switches that wouldn't change the world. What was I doing with my life?

I did take that trip and several others after it, (No dramatic running off the tarmac scene). But that moment launched me on a journey to find or create a life I believed in. It took years, painful mistakes and several course corrections. In fact, I don't think I'll ever be done learning and changing. But one thing I discovered while I was trying to find a good path for my life was that I was not alone; far from it.

When I shared the steps I was taking to change my life, friends and acquaintances looked at me with an expression of skepticism that tried to mask a mixture of longing and fear. They wanted to change their lives, too. How had I done it? Was it possible for them?

REINVENTION REPLACES RETIREMENT

Baby Boomers especially reacted this way. A lot of us were raised by parents who worked for the same company for decades. The ideal was to get into a good position and stay in the job 40 years until you retired with your gold watch.

But that was an ideal born out of a different time. Our parents lived through WWII and the Great Depression. Security and stability were paramount in their lives. For us, constant change has replaced the 40-year career. We also hunger for adventure. Baby Boomers are embracing adventure travel—you know, climbing Mt. Kilimanjaro—at a greater rate than any other group.

> *I like finding the most efficient and effective way of doing things. And I've learned that the most realistic approach is the Career Pivot: a series of half steps that gets you to your goal.*

Our parents had a life expectancy of 65. We can't even retire with full Social Security Benefits at 65 anymore because our life expectancy is closer to 80.

If we followed our parents' pattern, many of us would be on the verge of retirement. But most of us, thanks in part to economic downturn, have no retirement in sight. For some of us, our jobs have disappeared in industries that aren't coming back. For others, the job is still there but we can't stand the idea of doing it for two more decades.

That's how I wound up as a career design expert and starting Career Pivot. Whatever reason you have for wanting a change, you need a strategy, a logical plan. You need to know what challenges you're going to face and have a set of tools for overcoming them.

REINVENTION REQUIRES STRATEGY

I am a data guy who worked over 20 years for IBM and has years of experience training and teaching. I like systems. I like finding the most efficient and effective way of doing things. And I've learned that the most realistic approach is the Career Pivot: a series of half steps that gets you to your goal.

While making my own changes, and working with others on theirs, I've developed a pretty solid system. But if it's going to succeed for you, you will need to be really honest with yourself about where you are now. For example:

- What is your skill set?

- What are your resources? This includes a lot of things, such as financial resources as well as personal resources. When you make this change will your family be behind you? Do you have a support system?

- How is your health? This will impact what kind of career you can consider.

- What is your financial situation and what future financial needs can you anticipate?

- How do you feel about change?

- Are you ready to give this process whatever is required to get it done?

The last one is important. Picking a new direction for your life requires traveling uncomfortable new territory.

You will need to embark on a lot of introspection...who am I? How did I get here? Without this step, you might as well not bother, because you're likely to pedal hard to wind up in the same position you're in now.

You will have to stop being the expert with 20 years' experience and become the novice, asking for help. You may have to take courses, become smart about social media sites like Linked In, adjust your idea of what "the good life" is. If any of that sounds like a deal breaker, this may not be the moment for you to take the plunge.

But if it is the moment, I've got a set of tools to help you on your Career Pivot. Read on.

ACTION STEPS

✓ Will your family and friends support you in making a change? Go ask them!

✓ What barriers have prevented you from making career changes? Write down what you need to address them.

✓ Why now? Identify what has motivated you to read this book and take the first step in making a career change

RETIREMENT: GONE WITH THE WIND AND GOOD RIDDANCE

Baby Boomers embraced retirement like a religion. It was all the doctrines and fables wrapped up in a 401K: The ant and the grasshopper; sacrifice and paradise; work hard all your life, save your money in an IRA and receive your reward at the end. If you hate your job, retirement becomes that much sweeter. Keep your eyes on the day when, like the beautiful, silver haired couple in the retirement brochure, you'll be able to quit work and spend your days at the beach.

Of course, there was a chance we'd get hit by a meteor first. Or the economy could tank and take all our retirement savings with it. But those possibilities seemed remote.

For a lot of us, retirement became golden handcuffs, keeping us tied to careers where we had to drag ourselves to work every day and, once there, create diversions to distract us from the fact that we were there. Many of us were raised to stick to the safe path; avoid risk. I was one of those. Many of us were raised to move from the security of our parents' home into the security of a father-figure like solid company that would provide a structure for our success until we retired. We, in turn, would work hard and keep our noses clean.

THE DEATH OF THE 401K GOD

Then the economy did tank. Our great reward, our retirement, vanished almost overnight taking with it our entire vision of the future and flushing all our years of service to the 401K god. For people who love their careers, whose work suits their personalities and their lifestyles, evaporating retirement isn't such a problem. It's only a problem for people waiting to be set free from a career they drifted into. It's a problem for people whose industries have vanished or whose jobs have been sent overseas or given to machines.

For me, it wasn't the tanking economy, but a series of other financial and personal incidents that preceded the downturn that caused me to seriously reevaluate my path.

But for a long time, my path was the same as many of my contemporaries:

- Go to school
- Get a job that parents or counselors tell you will make you the best living according to the skill sets you've demonstrated thus far
- Get married
- Have kids
- Climb the ladder
- Buy increasingly expensive stuff that maxes out your annual salary increases. (This part we were really good at. We spent so much that our spending accounts for 70% of the US economy.)

It was supposed to lead to a happy ending. Bills paid. Kids educated, employed, successful, and producing grandkids.

We were supposed to sell the big house for a fat profit and pay cash for our beach condo. Travel the world or maybe buy an RV and spend our retirement touring America.

That was how it was supposed to go.

But that's not how it worked out.

THE NEXT ECONOMY WON'T
LOOK LIKE THE LAST ONE

Nobody really knew what was coming in June 2007 when the subprime mortgage market began to collapse. The last five years have been a series of catastrophic personal crashes for the Baby Boomers: losing jobs, homes, retirement savings, all the infrastructure of safety their parents had encouraged them to build since the 1950s.

More than seven million jobs have disappeared and an estimated three million will never come back. Many of those are in manufacturing and other industries where workers can be replaced more cheaply by technology or off shoring. Many were in the inflated housing market, building homes and selling mortgages. But that industry is forever changed. More than a million homes are in foreclosure.

Once upon a time, your house was your only sure investment. Now, a lot of homes are worth less than they were when the owners bought them. Many homeowners are trapped. They can't move to a city that has work because they can't sell their homes. Ironically, the cities with the largest percentage of home ownership—long considered a sign of stability—are now the cities struggling the most to emerge from the recession. Once, owning a home was an irrefutable pillar of the American Dream. Now, people are beginning to ask whether owning a home even makes sense any more.

Between plummeting home values and plummeting stocks, Boomers have lost about half their net worth since 2007 according to the Center for Economic and Policy Research. The Baby Boomers who counted on selling their businesses to retire, can't. Lending restrictions mean people can't get money to buy them.

> *Work has rewards beyond money. Work provides social interaction, structure and purpose. We use the skills we spent decades developing, while in retirement we wind up shelving them.*

On top of everything, more Baby Boomers are winding up with increasing personal responsibility. Many Boomers already knew they'd be caring for their aging parents but now a lot of Baby Boomers are raising their grandkids as well. The number of Baby Boomers raising their grandchildren has increased from 4.5 million to 4.9 million in the last ten years, according to the U.S. Census Bureau.

Even when the market picks up, we don't have decades to stash away retirement funds. Boomers need to face the new reality, go ahead and pitch a hissy fit—we're entitled—and move to Plan B.

PLAN B

Retirement is actually a newfangled idea. In the 1950's, very few people thought they could retire. People didn't live as long and more people worked physical jobs that didn't pay much. When you couldn't work anymore, you moved in with your children and waited to die. Then Social Security became widespread during the 1950's and Medicare was created in 1965. Suddenly it was everyone's prerogative to have a chunk of years where they enjoyed the fruits of their labor without working. Retirement quickly became an expectation. If you couldn't afford to retire, it reflected poorly on your ability to plan. But if you planned well, you could spend your final years on permanent vacation.

It sounded better than it was. The fact is, retirement is not really natural for most of us. Having been raised and trained to work all our lives, it doesn't track to suddenly have nowhere we have to be, no one we have to meet, and nothing that requires our expertise. Nobody wants to be obsolete. At IBM, in the 1990s it passed from rumor into adage that retirees—most of whom gave 30 plus years to the company--lived an average of 18 months after retiring. They were reputedly so wrapped up in being IBMers that when they lost that part of their identities, they just shriveled up.

I have this great old video about the first Sun City Retirement Community opening its doors in 1961. It shows a guy retiring, working on his house, swinging in his hammock, and growing increasingly lonely, bored and despondent. Then he discovers Sun City and a life of friends and activity. The video is hilarious in its kitschy quality, but it reveals a truth. People flocked to Sun City the minute it opened, desperately trying to escape their lives of inactivity.

REWARDS OF WORK BESIDES A PAYCHECK

Work has rewards beyond money. Work provides social interaction, structure and purpose. We use the skills we spent decades developing, while in retirement we wind up shelving them. We're contributing to the growth or success of something. We get rewards from being asked to take on more responsibility, to manage a tough project, even just getting a plaque or a pat on the back. Often, we don't realize how important those rewards are until they're gone. People who've lost their jobs understand the value.

Look at Mick Jagger who announced in 2010, at the age of 67, that he would retire in 2025. Why? The man has millions, fame, and a successful career behind him. He could have retired long ago, but he loves his work.

If you don't have a career you just can't bear to part with, it's time to find one. That "break" you were hoping for in retirement is gone. So how about looking, instead, for a career that fulfills you? One you can grow into for decades to come?

ACTION STEPS

- ✓ Throw yourself a "The Changing Economy Killed My Retirement" party. Clean up after. Move on.

- ✓ Write down what your retirement plans were before the economy collapsed versus now. What do the next 20, 30 years look like now?

- ✓ List the rewards you get from working, besides a paycheck.

TO GET WHAT YOU NEED YOU MUST KNOW WHAT YOU NEED

Most people are familiar with the Lewis Carroll paraphrase that "If you don't know where you're going, any road will get you there." But if you're tired of wandering around, never arriving at your goal, it's time to figure out a really clear destination.

So, on a granular level, what do you need from your job? This is a much bigger question than most people think. It's not just about pay, health care or even flex schedules. There's a host of underlying needs many of us never recognize. In fact, people are often really surprised by what assessments reveal about their deepest needs. Then, after a moment of reflection, the light goes on: "Oh, THAT's what that is! I never had a name for it before."

One woman, who thought she was immune to status, learned she REALLY valued aligning herself with key decision makers and knowing who was in charge of every project. When that didn't work out, she felt frustrated but she couldn't say why.

Many people, as I said before, really need to be in charge of their own schedules and organizational systems. If they can't, they're constantly frustrated.

Not getting what you need isn't always obvious, like having an abusive boss or unsanitary working conditions, but it can create low-grade anxiety and frustration all day, every day, that builds up.

You can transform your work life by seeking what you really need from the job—whether that's within your current occupation or in a new one. But you have to figure out what you need, and learn how to ask for it.

REWARDS

One of the top reasons we change jobs is because we do not feel valued. Most people want and need some kind of reward for doing good work. This can come in many forms:

- Pay increase

- Bonus check
- Public Recognition and Award
- Pat on the back and thanks from management
- Pat on the back and thanks from your peers
- Pat on the back and thanks from your customer

For me, the best reward is a pat on the back from my customer. After my epiphany with my bicycle accident, I became a high school math teacher. There, my customers were my students.

> *You can transform your work life by seeking what you really need from the job. But you have to figure out what that is, and learn how to ask for it.*

In case you haven't heard, students outside of After School Specials and Hallmark ads rarely thank their teachers. But in my second year, my previous year's students did come back and thank me for taking extra time, figuring out how to communicate in a way that was relevant, redefining rules to help them succeed.

That first year, working long days without ever getting the reward that met my needs was torture. I didn't understand my needs at the time so I couldn't put a finger on what was making life so stressful. In an urban school, on a new job, there are plenty of places to assign stress. Had I known what was really getting to me, I could have worked on coping mechanisms that would have helped a lot.

Some people, when they are most concerned about the reward of being recognized as a valuable team member, wind up not pushing for higher financial compensation. This can lead to inequalities in pay.

Some people are best rewarded by time off, more time for themselves.

What kind of reward system have you been accustomed to and how did it suit you? Was there a reward you wish you'd received more of?

FREEDOM

Freedom is...the ability to take a two-hour client lunch without explaining it to anybody; go to a doctor's appointment without a big hassle; take Friday afternoon off and make it up Saturday morning. Or, it can be the freedom to use your imagination in creating products and solutions. Or the freedom to wear jeans on the job, work from home or to speak your mind without multi-layered corporate censure. Really, freedom can be defined many ways. Most of them fall roughly into three areas:

- Freedom from supervisors constantly telling you how to do your job: micromanagement.

- Being creative and being individualistic in your approach.

- The level of structure and rules and who gets to create them.

I work with a lot of very experienced professionals who need all three. They want to do the job and for everyone else to get out of the way. As long as their results meet or exceed expectations, they don't want to answer to anyone.

This is actually a need that's being incorporated into some pioneering workplaces using the ROWE approach: Results Only Work Environment, where it's the work that matters—not where or when it's done.

If you could create your own job description in terms of freedom, what would it include?

RESPECT AND EMOTIONAL SUPPORT

When we go to work, we expect our peers to treat us in a way that makes us feel that we belong in the culture of the place where we work. Some of us prefer a culture where others talk to us very directly, with minimal emotion—just give me the facts. That communicates respect for our position.

Other people hate that way of communicating and want to be able to express when they're down or frustrated or excited about a project if they need to. Most people fall somewhere in between these two extremes.

How do we select jobs and environments where we will get the level of respect and emotional support we want and need? Through Strategic Networking, which we'll talk about in a later chapter, you can explore different environments for the level of directness in communication and the level of emotional support provided. You could ask someone who works at a company you're interested in about his or her supervisor's communication style.

Even if the person has a problem with the supervisor and is being careful about expressing it, you can usually read between the lines.

Look for keywords. If people talk about a "direct, no-nonsense, efficient and professional" style you can read that that's what they seek in a candidate. If the sound of that relaxes you, you might be a good fit. If, on the other hand, someone talks about a "warm, supportive, relational" workplace, you can bet that emotions are welcome there.

VARIETY

Do you like to multitask at work? One of the key happiness factors at work is how much variety you are afforded. I have many clients who NEED lots of variety and love to multitask. I, on the other hand, like steady work to do with very few interruptions.

Here are a few questions to ask yourself:

- Are you more or less productive when you have lots of things going on simultaneously? Many people instinctively say more. But are you sure?

- At what point does multitasking become stressful? Is it when you have three, five, ten, etc. things going on at the same time?

- What happens when you are interrupted frequently? Do you become stressed?

When I was teaching high school, my day was pretty regimented. I was doing the same thing all day. In my second year of teaching, I had five sections of Algebra II and therefore, I taught the same lesson five times. This would drive some people crazy but it fit well with my personality. My schedule was decided for me down to the minute. And that was okay because I got to be on my feet all day.

Again, that would drive some people crazy; but I can't sit at a desk for more than 45 minutes at a time. I loved the fact that I was on my feet and moving literally all day.

Think about what the perfect culture would be for you based on positive experiences and relationships you've had either at work, on teams or personally. These give you some good insights as to what your needs are.

Then you have to learn to ask for them.

ACTION STEPS

✓ Reflect back to the job or position when you felt most rewarded. What did you receive that made you feel good?

✓ Write down what you need from a job including such intangibles as freedom, respect, physical activity, variety.

✓ Write down the kind of culture you prefer to work in: small or large company, institutional or entrepreneurial, etc.

WHAT IS YOUR PERSONAL OPERATING SYSTEM?

Most of my clients have a whole system of needs, stressors and behaviors they are only marginally aware of. These things are constantly humming in the background, like the operating system of a computer. We don't think about them, but they impact everything about the way we feel and function.

One person, for example, might be extremely deliberate about making decisions. He researches every car on the market before buying one. He weighs every variable, constantly looking for opportunities or pitfalls others miss. It's how he's always been. Trying to make a decision faster makes him anxious. He worries about making mistakes that could have dire consequences.

At work, he gets frustrated with his boss who seems to expect him to do hours of research to prepare for questions she might throw at him at meetings. She wants input and decisions on issues he couldn't possibly have had time to weigh carefully.

In truth, she doesn't expect hours of research. She makes decisions quickly on the facts at hand and expects him to do the same. Such a thing would never dawn on him. It's too crazy, capricious, stressful. .....

He doesn't realize he needs a job where his thoroughness would be an asset. He just thinks he needs to get away from her.

That's what assessments are for.

FIRST STEP TO CAREER BLISS: KNOW THYSELF

Many of us go after jobs thinking "I want to get away from my boss; I want more money; I want to work for a bigger organization, or a smaller one." We think we've isolated the problem with our last job or career so we set out to solve the problem we identified.

But frequently, all we've really done is isolate a symptom, not the problem itself.

To find a career that will satisfy you in the long run, you need to understand many things about yourself: what you need, what stresses you and what makes you happy. Assessments reveal truths about us that we might not even think about as an issue in our careers. They can be the first step to understanding yourself--which is the first step to pursuing your own happiness and satisfaction.

I have done a bunch of assessments: MBTI (Meyers-Briggs), DISC, Kolbe, StrengthFinder 2.0, and Birkman. For me, the most valuable in gaining insight into my own needs was the Birkman.

When I took it, several years ago, I learned that I need plenty of alone time. I had no idea. I knew that, as a younger man, I'd been alone more than I liked. And I knew that I didn't enjoy my first job at IBM alone in a cubicle. I can also tell you I am quite social, I love to work a crowd and go to many gatherings every week. (In Austin, you could attend about a thousand a week if you had the time and stamina). What I didn't realize until I took the Birkman was that it's not an either/or. I didn't like being alone all the time. Nor could I just leap into constant social activity. I need a good balance of both.

That's a piece of information that could save me from many dissatisfying job changes. Without it, I could think: "I HATE being alone in my cubicle all day. I need a job where I'm working with people!" Next job, I'm in meetings, client calls or networking events from morning 'til night, exhausted and longing for my monastic cubicle.

That's the kind of thing the Birkman reveals. The Birkman is 298 fairly repetitious questions that ask what "I" do, think and believe and what I think "most people" do, think and believe.

For example, "Do you think it's more important to be honest than to avoid hurting people's feelings? Do you think others feel honesty is more important that protecting people's feelings?"

It's a strange test that, after being asked the same question about four different ways, can make you think "Who knows? Who cares? Why are you asking this again?"

But then, you sit down with a Birkman advisor who explains what your answers say about you. And suddenly it's like you're parked with a psychic who is telling you things that maybe you didn't want to know. But, to be honest, you sort of knew, deep down.

STEALTH COMPETITORS AND SENSITIVE ENGINEERS

Many of the women I work with, in fact, many women I talk to, are what I would call "Stealth Competitors." They were raised to believe that if they worked hard, people would recognize their contribution and reward them. These women would be characterized by their peers as very "sweet." They are affable, get along well with others, never hog the limelight. They just seem content to do their jobs. If asked, that's how they might describe themselves.

But the Birkman shows that these women are frustrated and angry. They don't understand why they're not getting recognition, praise and raises. The signals they're sending out—what the Birkman calls their "effective behavior"-- communicates that they are perfectly fine without the kinds of rewards other people receive. They may, in fact, have been hired because they seemed like someone who would ask very little. And that's what they get.

When they see those results, my clients always look shocked. "That's true!" they exclaim.

These women often don't realize that they are holding their bosses or clients to a code of behavior that says they should give kudos where kudos are due, even if the women don't seem to need them. The Birkman spells all of that out and a Birkman advisor would explain that these women need to ask for what they want. That's not always easy, as we'll talk about later. But it's crucial for these people's happiness.

I had another client who simply landed in the wrong career. In high school, he scored really high on the math portion of his PSAT and was told by a counselor: "Get thee to an engineering school." So he did.

Here's what the counselor didn't know, or think about: This guy is a very empathetic, emotional person. Most engineers are very low on the empathy scale. Over the years, he learned to act like his colleagues, but he was miserable. The Birkman confirmed in a clinical way that empathy wasn't a weakness in his work social skills, it was a strength he had to hide because of the environments he'd chosen. Now he could look for a career where both his engineering skills and his empathy would prove valuable.

ONE MAN'S HELL IS ANOTHER'S HEAVEN

A lot of men and women succeed in their fields because they are highly organized. They can easily prioritize tasks and focus their attention and energy where it will be most effective in that moment. These people aren't at all intimidated by having a lot to do, as long as they get to decide how to do it. But give a person like that a boss who is trying to "help" by writing out a detailed list of tasks and you will have one stressed out employee. The boss has, proverbially, just hobbled his best racehorse. The Birkman often exposes to these highly organized people that they must insist on a position where the culture or the boss will allow them to say: "Point me toward the goal and get out of my way." Then, watch 'em go!

If, on the other hand, you're someone who feels uncomfortable with a lot of autonomy and prefers to have your boss's and your company's expectations clearly spelled out so you don't have to make a lot of decisions, the boss with the detailed list would be ideal.

Some people function beautifully with a lot of distractions. They might be happy for coworkers to drop by with questions, listen to music while they work and switch easily from one quick task to the next.

Other people, me included, need stretches of uninterrupted work time to accomplish our best results. Being interrupted all the time shatters our thoughts and makes it almost too frustrating to get anything done. Some people, however, may not even realize that that's something they need to consider when looking at a job or career change. Is this a position where you could focus intensely for several hours or are you likely to be interrupted by customers or colleagues?

Spend time considering how you work best. In looking at salary and title, some people may not even realize that that's something they need to consider when looking at a job or career change. But it can make all the difference in the world in terms of job satisfaction and performance.

In July of 2010, I went on a grueling trip to Australia to teach a four-day sales class. At the end of each day, I had a group of the Aussie sales people who wanted to take me out for drinks. It would have been fun, but I knew I had to say no. I had a quiet dinner with a few close friends and went back to my room to watch the Tour De France. I knew this was what I had to do to properly take care of myself.

> *Many of us go after jobs thinking "I want to get away from my boss; I want more money; I want to work for a bigger organization...." Frequently, all we've done is isolate a symptom, not the problem itself.*

There are a number of remarkable things my clients have discovered from the Birkman. One woman found she was much happier in her job when she had a desk by the window and could bring plants to her work area.

Another client discovered that it really upset her when someone with less expertise stepped in on decisions about her part of a project. After taking her assessment and learning the results, she knew she would still have her expertise challenged, but she recognized it and was able to devise ways to handle it more gracefully.

It took me months to internalize the information I learned about myself in the Birkman report, with the help of my adviser. I still go back, review my report and I STILL am learning about myself.

There was a great article in Fortune Magazine in 2010 that was reprinted by CNN Money on the value of the Birkman called "Are You a Good Fit for Your Job?"

Senior Editor Jennifer Reingold learned—among other things-- that, while she's keen on taking the direct approach with others, she's not too thrilled about it when she's on the receiving end.

What could a Birkman or similar assessment tell you that would set you on, not just a new path or a different path, but on the right path?

ACTION STEPS

✓ Take a career assessment test, such as the Birkman, to uncover rules and motivators you didn't even know you had-- Your personal Operating System. Schedule an assessment by contacting me at : www.careerpivot.com/birkman.

WHEN THE CLOUDS PART: MOMENTS OF CLARITY

Can you remember a moment when the assorted junk that plagues your mind—your controlling boss, your extra 15 pounds, the ugly tile in your bathroom or your battle over which one of you gets a new car--suddenly vanish in the face of something life altering? It might be your child is sick, or your spouse, or you. It might be a death in the family, a divorce, a layoff or a natural disaster. It might even be good news, like an inheritance or an opportunity.

Whatever it is, it suddenly turns your perspective upside down.

I call these Moments of Clarity.

Suddenly the way you were living doesn't make sense. You think to yourself, "Why did I ever think that ugly tile was important? Why did I spend so many sleepless nights over that argument? Why didn't I pursue my dreams? How did I not see the truth before?"

A Moment of clarity may or may not touch on your career. But if it does, it reveals truths you've been ignoring or deliberately hiding from yourself.

You might realize that your parents pushed you into a career you didn't want, or that the company you work for has institutional barriers that will never let you succeed.

You might see that you always wind up with narcissistic bosses and wonder what that is about. Or you might realize you habitually undermine yourself, selling yourself short to more powerful colleagues.

Because of a dramatic—if temporary—change in circumstances, nothing looks the same as it did yesterday. The filters that prevented you from seeing things as they are have come down and you have an opportunity to learn something about yourself.

You learn what is really important to you at those times.

The problem is, those filters go back up quickly. The moment passes and next thing you know, the bathroom tile is bugging you again. If you don't act in that moment of clarity, or set a change in place, you'll go on as you were with a nagging sense of missed opportunity.

> *If you don't act in that moment of clarity, or set a change in place, you'll go on as you were, with a nagging sense of missed opportunity.*

I am happy to say I can see many times I acted in a moment of clarity and was always better for it.

For example:

- When I got married. I have been married for 30 years to my lovely bride Lotus. The first year was difficult. I learned an immense amount about myself and what I wanted in life and a relationship.

- The day my son was born. The following year was amazing and I made a lot of personal changes during that time.

- When I got hurt. In December of 1992, I ruptured the L4/L5 discs in my lower back. I either had to get an operation or take three months off on disability to recover. I chose to take the time off. I'd always overloaded myself with projects and now I was forced to relax.

In the process, I discovered peace. All my previous stress seemed so unnecessary in light of this revelation of being calm. Simple things became delightful.

When I went back to work at IBM, the company was near bankruptcy and my familiar, stressed-out colleagues were panicked about being unable to afford their bloated lifestyles. But I saw clearly that I didn't want to swap my newfound peace with this anxiety again.

I was willing to make whatever changes necessary to my career and lifestyle to preserve my contentment.

- My bicycle accident left me wondering why I was placed on this earth. I then planned my career pivot to teaching high school math.

The thing is, whatever you learned in that Moment of clarity is still in you, somewhere, though it no longer takes a front seat in your awareness. And it still has things to teach you.

So when I work with clients, I always have them go back and look for moments of clarity in their lives. I have them chronicle each one and what it taught them.

Then, because these moments might not be as dramatically clear in a career situation, I have them go back and chronicle information about every job they've ever held.

You'd be amazed at the patterns that emerge. Try this. Fill out your own job history using these criteria.

START OF JOB

- Description: Briefly summarize the job and its duties.

- Reason You Took this Job:

- Influenced By: Who or what influenced you to take this job?

- How You Found This Job: Colleague? Online site? Headhunter?

- Environment: What was the environment of this place?

- Feel: How did the environment make you feel?

- Team or Solo: Were you part of a team or were you on your own? What was your role? Were you the team leader or a participant? How well did the team function? Did you like being on this team?

- Independence: Were you free to control how you did your job, or were the rules created for you?

- Manager's Style: What was the management style of your supervisor?

- Work Pace/Schedule: Did you have control of your schedule? How varied were your activities during the course of a day? How much physical activity did this job require?

- Rewards: Did you feel valued? If so, what actions by your employer demonstrated to you that your contribution was valued?

- Best Thing About This Job:

- Worst Thing About This Job:

- What I Learned About What I Needed:

- What I Learned About What I Do Not Need:

END OF JOB
- Reason You Left This Job:

- Who or What Influenced You to Leave:

- Exit Status: Did you have another job to go to when you left?

If you do this for every position or job you have ever had and put them in order I will almost guarantee you will see a pattern. Most of us have made the same mistakes in our careers more than once. I call this Career Insanity or doing the same thing over and over but expecting a different outcome each time.

Moments of clarity are moments when your perception shifts. You're likely to have one after reflecting back on your life and your career. You're likely to see patterns and missed opportunities that have brought you to where you are now.

Take this as a moment of clarity. What do you want to do from today on?

ACTION STEPS

✓ Retrace moments in your life when you suddenly saw life differently. These could be because of a problem, like an illness or layoff or something good, like marriage or the birth of a child.

✓ Write down what you learned in these moments, whether you followed the lessons they taught or ignored them, and what the results were.

✓ Retrace your job history. What did you learn about yourself and your needs from each of the jobs you've held?

OUT OF THE FRYING PAN AND INTO THE FIRE: FANTASY JOBS

I blame it on movies like *Stand and Deliver*, *To Sir with Love*, *Freedom Writers*: everybody wants to be a teacher. Moreover, they want to be teachers in an inner-city school full of kids with hard lives so they can make a difference. Okay, maybe not everybody, but it's definitely one of those romanticized careers people pursue like being a baker, or a landscaper. They imagine the wounded kid from the bad family getting a scholarship to Harvard because of their efforts. Or listening to Bach while they whip up delightful pastries that taste and smell heavenly. Or planting azaleas in a quiet garden on a sunny day when it's 70 degrees outside.

That's the problem with just jumping from one job to another. We romanticize the pleasant parts and make assumptions about the rest. For example, I assumed it would be easy for me to become a teacher. I had an engineering degree and I had been professionally training people all over the world.

Really, I figured school districts would fight over me. I was wrong.

When I was pursuing my degree 20 years before, I managed to avoid ALL English classes. I had multiple learning disabilities and English was torture for me. I felt triumphant when I graduated without having to suffer much reading. But after all I had accomplished, those missing English hours caused me to be ineligible for the alternative teaching certification program offered by the state.

I was stunned. Here I was, with all my credentials, competing against a bunch of green kids and being asked about my activities from the 1970s! They wanted contact information for my first supervisor (I imagined my immediate supervisor from that job was long gone—he'd been in his 50s and a heavy smoker more than 20 years ago.)

They asked for my college transcripts. Transcripts! Why not my first grade report card?

REALITY BITES

So I was rejected for the certification program. Once I recovered from that blow, I decided I wasn't beaten yet and entered the Alternative Certification program at the local community college.

School districts, incidentally, did not fight over me either. I got a job because I had a friend who turned down an opening and told me about it, giving me a chance to send my application in first.

There were other surprises in store for me. I assumed school districts would have good health benefits and I could enroll myself, my wife and my son for far less than I was paying for my COBRA health insurance policy from my previous employer. WRONG. The school district contributed $250 a month for the teachers' health insurance and nothing for children and spouse. My monthly contribution would be double my COBRA payment. My monthly deduction was over $1,000 a month. My take home was only $2,500 a month, before benefits were taken out.

I assumed my teaching experience with adults would translate to teaching kids or at least that my experience with having a high school-aged son would translate. They didn't. Nothing prepared me for the kinds of violence and indifference of the kids I taught. The frame of reference this group of kids shared was so foreign to me that my trips to corporate China seemed familiar by comparison.

> *Happiness comes from the intersection of what you love, what you're good at, and what the world needs—Harvard Business Review*

Moreover, I was doing something new every day for a year. It never got easier. The second year I followed another teacher's lesson plans to a tee, but I had shifted from teaching Algebra I to Algebra II. Again, every day, I taught something brand new. There were a million opportunities for failure.

Ultimately, I realized the stress would kill me if I stayed.

Here's the thing: In some ways, I grew to love being a teacher. I figured out how to make algebra easier for my students. I figured out how to talk to them and even challenge them in a way that they could listen to.

Ninety percent of my kids could not add 8 plus 3 in their heads. So, how was I going to teach them to factor quadratic equations? I taught them to use the TI graphing calculators to do everything. I focused on the muscle memory in their fingers so they instinctively would move their fingers across the keypad solving problems.

Being a child of the 60's I used Sex, Drugs and Rock and Roll to get them to listen. I spent one day a month on simple life skills like buying a used car, how to rent an apartment, and the difference between a debit and credit card.

My first year of teaching was incredibly success-ful. I had more than doubled the passing rates on the standardized end of year exams compared to previous years. No one in the administration noticed. I wish I could say the knowledge that I was helping those kids was enough for me. But while I was helping them, I couldn't save them from the difficult home lives or street lives or other issues they faced. And there was always a new wave of kids I had to win over each year.

My body was falling apart with aches, pains and illness and I knew what it was trying to tell me. I had to leave teaching to survive.

The experience taught me one of the hardest lessons I've ever learned: Before you drop everything and jump into a career, you need to understand the career. It's not enough to be passionate.

THE PITFALLS OF PASSION

On January 13th, 2012, the Harvard Business Review published a blog post titled "To Find Happiness, Forget About Passion." The HBR blog post was about how the current twenty-somethings have been following their passion, unlike the generation before them who rarely even considered passion.

But the article pointed out that just swinging the pendulum the other way wasn't necessarily a good idea either. There was more to consider. The closing statement said:

"Happiness comes from the intersection of what you love, what you're good at, and what the world needs. We've been told time and again to keep finding the first. Our schools helped develop the second. It's time we put more thought on the third."

The world needs good teachers and passion is a key ingredient. But are you good at dealing with people who need you all day every day to be a teacher, mentor, babysitter, surrogate parent? I wasn't.

In leaving that job I was leaving something I'd poured sweat and tears into, believing it was my purpose. Giving up on that nearly crushed me and sent me into a depression for a while.

So while you're on your journey for a new career, think about your passion, your skills and what the world needs. But make sure that before you dive too deep into anything, you talk to people who have walked the road you're thinking of walking. And when they tell you the down side, listen, don't gloss over it.

Bakers have to be at work at 4 a.m. and can't stay out at night when the rest of the world is socializing. Landscapers have to plant azaleas when it's 110 in the shade.

Don't waste time pursuing a career you may wind up hating. Before you take many steps in any direction, you MUST strategically network and find out what it's really like out there.

You may find out your dream job isn't what you thought. But that just puts you one step closer to the right path, without a costly detour.

ACTION STEPS

- ✓ Write down a list of jobs that seem to you to be "dream jobs."

- ✓ Research the pros and cons of these jobs. For example, if you want to be a gardener, you get to work outside but must be outside even in bad weather.

- ✓ If you are seriously considering any of these "dream jobs," find someone in the business you can talk to about the pros and cons, politics, physical demands and so forth.

- ✓ Be tough on yourself. Don't gloss over the cons or you'll wind up in the same spot.

WHY ARE YOU REALLY LEAVING?

A lot of us can be happy doing so-so tasks for adequate pay if we really like the people we work with. If, when you get to work in the morning, you feel like you're surrounded by friends who will do their work and support you doing yours and if you all like and respect the boss, everything else can be gravy. But what if you hate the people you work with?

If you're thinking about leaving your position, is it because of the team or the boss? If so, you need to analyze specifically what bugs you before making the leap.

In the late 1990's, I left a very comfortable position working at an IBM customer briefing center to make a career pivot to be an IT consultant. I had grown bored with the position at the briefing center and IBM was becoming a riskier place to invest my career over time. I felt if I got back to my technical roots I would be happier, but more importantly safer.

Boy was I wrong!

I was assigned to develop a point-of-sale solution for a national short-term loan company. The more I learned about the industry, the less I liked working on the project.

I was also surrounded by full time consultants who were unhappily single, unhappily married or divorced. New consultants rotated in every few weeks to support the project. About three months in, I found myself feeling pretty isolated and lonely. I really missed the strong and supportive relationships I had at the briefing center. Nine months later, my young project manager tried to publicly humiliate me and I quit the project and the consulting group.

THE TEAM

I had a couple of months to find a position within IBM or be let go. I found one in marketing but I knew that was just a holding spot for me while I started to explore what I really wanted to do next, so I decided to return to training. But the training opportunities that existed at IBM would have taken me away from Austin. That wouldn't do.

So I left IBM after 22 years and was hired by Agere Inc, a semiconductor high tech startup. What I did not know at the time was I was walking into an environment that was the polar opposite of the consulting environment. We had a great team and virtually no office politics. Most of us stayed on long after the company was acquired by Lucent because it was such a supportive environment.

One common theme I find with clients who are very experienced professionals is they want a manager to support them but to get the heck out of their way so that they can get the job done.

Each career step I've taken has demonstrated and validated that the team I work with is extremely important to me. As a solo entrepreneur, I purposely created a supportive team around me. I have found this is crucial to my success and, more importantly, to my happiness.

What is the team environment like in your current position? Is there anything you can do to make it better? What type of team environment is right for you?

List the three characteristics that you most value in a team.

THE BOSS

Sometimes you can have a great team around you, but you're living under the thumb of a terrible boss. Before you make a career or job change, you have to get real clear about what your manager does to make your life miserable so you don't go out and find the same type of situation:

- Is your boss a micro-manager? One common theme I find with my clients who are very experienced professionals is they want a manager to support them but to get the heck out of their way so that they can get the job done.

- Is your boss a wimp? Does he or she just keep dumping work on you that comes from above so that you're overworked?

- Is your boss selfish? Is he or she focused on looking good for upper management but disinterested in the career advancement of you and your teammates?

- Is your boss abusive? Does your manager take advantage of people by verbally or emotional abusing them?

Once you figure out what the boss is doing wrong, it's easier to make a definite list of what you want in a boss.

CONTROL

Studies over several decades have shown that job satisfaction is directly related to employees' ability to control how they work. Do you get to make decisions about your own area of expertise or is everything dictated? If you see places where work flow could be improved in your area, for example, is your input welcomed or discouraged?

Structure about rules is another issue. Some people are fine with rigid work hours and rules about conduct, numbers of hours in the office, dress, the format of documents and everything else. Other people don't mind working hard as long as they have the freedom to make their own rules about when they work, where they work, how they dress and so on.

PHYSICAL ACTIVITY LEVEL

Most of us have now learned that spending all day at a desk slows our metabolism way down and is hard on our backs. However, some people have physical issues that make it impossible to be on their feet or moving all day. Physical activity level can make or break a job.

I'm one of those people who are up and around all of the time. When I took a position as an IT consultant where I was sitting in a cubicle all day, it drove me nuts; I could not do it. I am the guy who attends class and after a few hours is standing in the back; I cannot sit for hour after hour. I love to be out talking to people.

You can take all these aspects of work and map them back to different positions you've held to identify why you were not happy.

REWARDS

I talk a lot about rewards because it is one of the key elements to happiness. Are you getting the right rewards? Were you looking for money but got pats on the back? Were you looking to be assigned more challenging projects but ended up with a gift certificate?

ORGANIZATIONAL STRUCTURE

I work with two very creative and artistic women. Both have left the corporate world where they had varying levels of success but little happiness. They all have one major similarity on their assessments, their organizational focus—that is, how well they fit into traditional corporate roles and responsibilities. They're lone rangers.

The Birkman Assessment's Organization Focus section has four bars that compare your answers to questions with the answers of people who are successful in various job classifications. If your bar on this chart is wide, it means that your responses match closely with those who are successful in various careers. That indicates you might be happy and successful in those careers too. The categories are defined by the Department of Labor.

Here is my organizational focus report. I am a chameleon who has worked in training, sales, teaching and IT:

Similarity to others in this job arena:	Intensity	Intensity
Green - Sales/Marketing		
Yellow - Admin/Fiscal		
Blue - Design/Strategy		
Red - Operations/Technology		

But the artistic, creative women I work with who used to work in the corporate world, their charts look like this:

Similarity to others in this job arena:	Intensity	Intensity
Yellow - Admin/Fiscal		
Red - Operations/Technology		
Green - Sales/Marketing		
Blue - Design/Strategy		

Similarity to others in this job arena:	Intensity	Intensity
Yellow - Admin/Fiscal		
Red - Operations/Technology		
Green - Sales/Marketing		
Blue - Design/Strategy		

Notice their bars are very narrow. This means that how they answered the questions was vastly different from people who are successful in these categories such as administration, sales and marketing and operations. They do not appear to be good fits at all for these areas.

These women are now solo-entrepreneurs, successful and happy. None of them fit the corporate mold. Why did they ever enter Corporate America? They are all Baby Boomers who were raised to be employees and work for paternal and father-like companies. They did what they believed they were expected to do.

When I taught high school math, I experienced the same with my students. My very creative and artistic kids were screwed by the public school system. They did not learn in the same regimented way as other students. They did not fit in the system.

How about you? How well do you fit the corporate mold? Would you be happier outside of corporate America?

If so, what stops you?

I've gone over several areas that help you figure out what you DON'T want. The next step is to understand what you DO want, and how to get it.

ACTION STEPS

- ✓ Make a list of why you want to leave this job, and why you've left others. Is it the boss? (It usually is) The organizational structure? The workplace environment?

- ✓ Try to break down what, about those issues is driving you away? If you're not clear, you could wind up in the same soup in the next job.

- ✓ Spell out, in writing, how you want the next situation to be different.

THE HARDEST PART: ASKING FOR HELP

Believe it or not, often the hardest part of shifting careers or making changes within your career is asking for help.

I admit it – I am a guy. I do not like asking for help. I do not like asking for directions. There, I said it. Sometimes, we're thrust into situations where our choices are to quit or ask for help. Admit it, you have been there!

You can't do this alone. No matter how many books, articles, or blogs you read, you will have to talk to real people in the world you're seeking to enter.

The people in your industry or the company you are targeting are the ones who can tell you about the top players in the industry, the unspoken rules, and the most tested paths to success.

They're the ones who can introduce you to the right people, put in a good word for you or steer you away from the kinds of people who can sabotage your efforts.

A LITTLE HUMBLE PIE WITH YOUR COFFEE?

In these transactions, you're the receiver, the seeker, the newbie, not the expert. The lunch you bought your source doesn't adequately compensate him or her for the knowledge you're getting and you're not in the power position. That's hard for people who have achieved success in their careers and a certain number of gray hairs on their heads.

For most of us guys, it can actually be a pretty miserable experience. I was a very experienced professional. I was successful in whatever I had done in my career. I had never really failed miserably at anything until I got the teaching gig. When I did fail miserably there, I wanted to just quit.

Because I didn't believe I should quit, I sucked it up and asked for help. It was hard. But it was eye opening and I ended up being an almost religious supporter of the notion that people really only get where they're going with the help of other people.

Here's the shocker: Most people are happy to help you. For one thing, people generally like to be helpful.

> *I ended up being an almost religious supporter of the notion that people really only get where they're going with the help of other people*

For another, you are offering them the power position and that feels good to everyone. Think of giving the other person that role as a gift. As long as you pay the tab for the coffee or the meal and send them a thank you note later on, both of you will wind up benefiting from your session.

And it gets easier. Not everyone will have insights that move you forward, but just practicing asking for help is an enormously powerful thing.

There are several areas where Baby Boomers may need help:

RESEARCHING POTENTIAL CAREERS

- Asking someone on the inside, what it's really like to work in a specific field.

- Asking someone on the inside what it's like to work for a specific company, and what it takes to get in and succeed.

- Asking for advice about what's needed in a specific career.

- Asking for a recommendation or introduction to someone who can give you more advice.

SEEKING SUPPORT

- Asking for a recommendation on your resume or Linked In.

- Asking for someone to put in a good word for you.

SOCIAL MEDIA HELP

I know many Baby Boomers who are extremely social media savvy. But I still meet Baby Boomers who treat social media like some 'newfangled thing for the kids.' If that's you, it's time to get over it.

These days, there are dozens of online tools for everything from scheduling a meeting with someone to organizing business contacts. Sophisticated and successful companies use social media like Facebook, Twitter and Linked In as much or more than they use the telephone. Many companies don't even use resumes any more, they use Linked In instead.

Somebody may ask you to use Timebridge or Doodle to set up an appointment. They may want to connect with you on Facebook or Google Plus. Many Baby Boomers have chosen to ignore these new mediums so they don't have to feel embarrassed about not knowing how to use them. Sorry, you're going to have to learn to use them.

This is one area where you may need help either from an expert or a savvy friend, on how to use these tools to present yourself as competent in the current business climate.

ALL IS NOT LOST

Probably, the skills and experience you've amassed over your career will find a place in your new career and help you be even better at your new job than you would have been without them.

But right now, clinging to the security of competency you've demonstrated at your old job will just get in the way of finding a new career you can enjoy for the next several decades.

Depending on the magnitude of the pivot you intend to make, you will have to suck it up and be humble. You are no longer the expert. I have a friend who is making a major change into green energy. He is working as an apprentice electrician. He is learning to be humble.

When he's done, he'll have new knowledge that will take him into a future he wants, coupled with everything he's learned about working hard, meeting customers' expectations, and marketing himself.

He will have made the Pivot. After all, that's the goal.

ACTION STEPS

✓ List areas where others can help, such as making connections for you, giving you the scoop on certain industries or companies, bringing your social media up to date.

✓ Find people who can help you reach those goals and connect with them via Linked In, email or phone call.

✓ Take these people out for coffee, lunch or a walk. Remember to be humble. This time, you're not the expert!

BUILDING YOUR TRIBE

Networking is the way everything works. It's the old: "It's not what you know, it's who you know." But exchanging business cards and a Linked In connection is just scratching the networking surface.

People with whom you share that kind of superficial relationship are unlikely to impact your career, or your Career Pivot. The people who make a difference are your Tribe. A tribe is the difference between quantity and quality of your network. It's fine to have 500+ Linked In connections.

But it's crucial to have a group of people with whom you have actual relationship, who are interested in helping you reach your goals and depending on you to help them reach theirs. I have a rather large network, but my tribe consists of about 150 people.

Your tribe is the group of people who will get you through your Career Pivot, because believe me, with all this change, facing uncertain prospects and being humble while asking for help, you are going to need some people rooting for you. Your tribe is also the group you can call on for an introduction or some advice over coffee. And they can call on you, too--whether for themselves, or for a friend who wants some intelligence about your areas of expertise. It's like the barn raising communities where you all help your neighbor build his barn, knowing—without asking-- he'll show up with lunch and a hammer to help you raise yours.

A TRIBE WILL GET YOU THROUGH THIS

When I was a teacher, I began sending out regular emails about my experiences with the kids. I talked about the kids who seemed overwhelmed and the strategies I devised to help them. I talked about their low self esteem and the issues they were struggling to overcome, and how hard it was to communicate something as abstract as algebra in the midst of their concrete problems. I learned that many people I sent those emails to forwarded them to friends and family members in the school district. I unwittingly built a tribe of people who were rooting for me, and for my kids, throughout those hard years. I couldn't have made it without them.

Don't try to do something as challenging as a Career Pivot without a tribe.

CULTIVATE YOUR TRIBE

The thing about a tribe is, you have to cultivate it, like a garden. You need to weed it from time to time of people you have no real connection with. You have to water it when there's no rain. You may need to apply fertilizer. Most importantly, you should not neglect it. You need to cultivate a habit of giving it Tender Loving Care (TLC). It needs to be part of the way you think and live, or it will wither.

Do you have friends you have not seen in months? Take a day each week to reach out with an e-mail and check in. At least once a week, I glance through Linked In or Outlook contacts and find someone I have not heard from in a while. I send them my checking in e-mail.

It could be as simple as:

Bob,
I have not heard from you in a while. How are you doing? How is your family? Things are going well with my business. Son is getting married in October...
Let me know how you're doing and do you want to meet for a cup of coffee sometime soon?
Marc

The response is often:

Marc,
Thanks for checking in with me. Life is good...
Too busy to meet for coffee but check back in...
Bob

I now know how he is doing and he knows that I care about him. Networking is all about building relationships. Are you cultivating your network? Are you doing something new and original that you would like to share?

There is no substitute for face-to-face meetings to establish and maintain relationships. I like social media, but that good old face-to-face meeting where you get to shake hands and read body language is critical to long-term relationships.

When do you have the time to do this?

MAKE IT A HABIT

I like to have coffee meetings first thing in the morning at 7 or 7:30 AM. When our son was small, I learned it was easy for me to keep that hour clear for networking. My wife, boss, team-mates, and son could schedule things for me to do at any other time. But first thing in the morning was sacred. Sometimes it is not to meet for coffee. In Austin, where I live, people often meet while walking around Lady Bird Lake in the center of town. It might even be for a game of tennis or similar sport. No matter what I'm doing, it's about the connection.

What time works for you? Lunch, after work for a beer or other libation, or maybe Saturdays?

Pick a time, once a week, once every two weeks or once a month, to meet face to face with someone in your network. Make it a pattern.

LET KARMA DO ITS THING

When you network, it is all about the other person and you should expect nothing in return. When I am meeting with someone and if I determine I can be of some help, I just do it.

Recently, I met with my image consultant, Jean LeFebvre, to order a new shirt. Jean told me she was looking for companies who cared about how their employees dressed and would be willing to hire someone to make them look spiffy. In Austin, casual is king and there aren't many options. The one industry we could agree met her criteria was lawyers. Austin is the state capital; we have lots of lawyers.

> *Cultivating good karma as a habit will always pay off somewhere. Don't ask for it, it will happen in a way that's better than what you might have asked for.*

I offered to introduce Jean to Susan Baughman who has a business called "Lawyers Don't Know Marketing". Susan creates custom marketing programs for law firms, a rather unique business.

I sent Susan an e-mail, in which the subject line was "Virtual Introduction" and I copied Jean. I explained the situation and asked Susan if she could help Jean. As it turns out, Susan was looking for an image consultant for her clients and was willing to educate Jean on the art of dealing with law firms in Austin.

Making this kind of connection isn't just a fluke. Part of cultivating your tribe is looking for opportunities to do things like this for other people and not expecting anything in return. It's good will, good karma. Somewhere down the road, it will come back to you.

In the situation I mentioned about connecting my two friends, one of them may one day be dealing with an attorney who wants to make a career shift and instead of just listening sympathetically to the attorney's frustration, she'll send them an introduction them to me. Who knows? The point is, cultivating good karma as a habit will always pay off somewhere.

Don't ask for it, it will happen in a way that's better than what you might have asked for.

DON'T FORGET TO SAY THANK YOU

If someone makes a connection for you, though, don't forget to send a quick note or email to tell them what happened and thank them.

Dear Barb,
Thank you so much for introducing me to Stephen. We have connected over coffee and found several places where our business objectives might lead to really fruitful partnerships.
I don't know if we would have ever discovered each other without your help. Thanks for taking the time to do that!
Leslie

People don't need a reward for helping you. But you should give them the gift of letting them know that they did, in fact, help.

Building your tribe, cultivating it and giving it TLC might be the most valuable and enriching part of making a Career Pivot.

ACTION STEPS

✓ Connect regularly with members of your Tribe, friends and associates. They provide emotional support and may have leads for you.

✓ Thank them promptly with a note for any help they give you and let them know the outcome of their help.

✓ Seek ways to help others in their career or business goals without asking anything in return. Karma works.

HOW TO NETWORK STRATEGICALLY

What the heck is strategic networking? It is networking with a defined goal and a strategy to get to that goal. For example:

- You are unemployed and your goal is a job in a specific company that pays well and treats employees well. Your strategy might be to cozy up to the recruiter or hiring manager for a specific company.

- Your goal is a career change. Your strategy is to meet professionals in the field that you wish to switch into, with a goal to decide on a new career path.

- Your goal is to move up or laterally in your current company. Your strategy is to meet and build relationships outside of your current management chain.

Strategic networking is building relationships with people who can help you obtain that next professional position. They might be in a specific industry or even a specific company within that industry. The strategic part is finding contacts in those industries or companies who can connect you with new contacts. These might be employees, executives or recruiters.

NETWORKING WITH A RECRUITER

Having connections with multiple recruiters is useful in your job search but also in managing your career. Recruiters go from company to company, moving with hiring trends, this is particularly true of contract recruiters, and they carry their connections with them. Don't be intimidated to approach recruiters. They have this job because they like helping people find jobs that work.

> *Strategic networking is building RELATIONSHIPS with people who can help you obtain that next professional position.*

Recruiters are usually connected on Linked In to the vast majority of the personnel within the organizations they support. They also accept links to potential candidates readily. One last point about recruiters is the e-mail addresses they use with Linked In are usually the company's e-mail address. This allows you to understand how the corporation formats their e-mail addresses. If you only have the employee name you should be able to figure out his or her e-mail address.

Next, locate a recruiter at the target company and connect with him or her. If you are a viable candidate, they will want to connect. If they do not connect, try a different recruiter at the same company. If the recruiter does connect, call her. And here's what you say:

- If you are looking at a specific job, ask which recruiter is handling the position.
- If you are looking at a specific area within the company, ask which recruiter is handling that specific area.

- Ask about the culture and opportunities within the company.

- If he/she does not answer, leave a message with your questions and follow up with an e-mail. Be persistent and repeat this procedure in a few days if you don't get a response.

STRATEGIC NETWORKING WITH AN INDIVIDUAL

So what if you want to meet an individual in a company who might be able to help you reach your goals? Let's say his name is Jeffrey. Do you contact Jeffrey and ask him for an "informational interview?" That's how some people do it. But I don't like the term "informational interview." It says I want a JOB which scares people off.

INSTEAD, ASK FOR A – I – R

- A – Advice – When you ask for advice it is a compliment. Rarely will anyone turn you down when you ask advice. In the e-mail, ask for 30 minutes of Jeffrey's time to ask for some advice. It could be about how to pursue a position at the company or to learn more about the company. The magic word is "advice!"

- I – Insights – Once you meet Jeffrey, ask for his insights into how the company functions, the culture and management structure.

- R – Recommendations – This is what many people forget. Ask "What should I do next? Is there anyone else you would recommend I talk with? Can you introduce me to anyone else within the organization?"

You will ask Jeffrey questions and only talk about yourself when asked.

You have not asked for help to get a job, only for help in understanding the organization and for further networking opportunities. You are networking to build relationships and not to find a job. The opportunity to interview for a position will come later, after you have established relationships. Jeffrey will likely provide an introduction to at least one person, if not two, if you made it clear you were interested in him and his perspective.

Again, this is not about you!

ABOUT CONNECTORS

Some people pride themselves on being connectors, I am one such person. We're not recruiters or HR people; we just enjoy helping people along their career paths and we're good at making relationships with a lot of different people.

We attend a lot of functions, eagerly meet new associates, and remember to pull out your name when we hear someone speaking about needing someone with your skills, attributes or background.

We are worth cultivating because our hobby is so helpful to other people. If you know someone you think is a connector, take the time and trouble to take that person to coffee and ask for AIR. Who knows what it will lead to?

NEXT STEP, SEND THANK YOU NOTES

Never forget to send thank you emails as you move forward in your strategic networking.

- Send a thank you note to Ann who introduced you to Jeffrey. Ann will want to know the outcome of your meeting with Jeffrey.

- Send a thank you note to Jeffrey.

- Jeffrey introduces you to Paul. After you meet with Paul, you should do the following:

- Send a note to Jeffrey to let him know the outcome of your meeting with Paul.

- Send a note to Ann to let her know that you met with Paul.

- Send a thank you note to Paul.

If Paul introduces you to Mary, after meeting with Mary you send a note to Ann, Jeffrey, Paul, and Mary. After each meeting you send a note to everyone who helped you get there.

Yes, EVERYONE.

It really bugs me when I make an introduction for someone and I find out six months later that it led them down a chain of events that had a positive outcome and no one told me. Please come back and tell me.

Strategic networking is building RELATIONSHIPS with people who can help you obtain that next professional position.

If you go back and thank the person who helped you, you deepen the relationship.

Frequently, the only benefit the person who helped you derives from the interaction is the knowledge he helped someone. But that is a great feeling. It releases dopamine, a brain chemical connected with reward. It gives him a boost in his day. And it keeps him from wondering if he made a terrible mistake. Let him know what happened.

Moreover, as you progress forward, you might make a connection that is helpful to the people who helped you get there.

Don't be surprised if you, the person asking for help, very quickly becomes the one offering it.

ACTION STEPS

✓ Network with recruiters and individuals—especially people who like to be Connectors--who can help you toward your goals through Linked In and networking events.

✓ Don't ask for an informational interview or even for help finding a job. Instead, buy them lunch or coffee and ask only for Advice, Insights and Recommendations: AIR.

✓ Thank everyone who helps and let them know the outcome of their help.

HOW JOB HUNTING
IS LIKE DATING

Managing your career is a lot like dating and marriage. This is coming from a guy who has been married for over 30 years. Everyone assures me that I'm not missing anything... I really do not want to date again.

Frequently, we date the same way we look for a job: We put our best foot forward and pray they won't reject us. If that's all you're doing, if you aren't also deciding whether you really want to be stuck with them, you can wind up with some lousy partners...and jobs.

Every date does not turn into marriage and it's only after lots of dates, when you are sure that the two of you are compatible, that it turns into a good marriage. The same thing happens when you go in for an interview.

Another similarity: Waxing bitter about your previous relationships will not produce good results. If you complain about your current managers, just like if you gripe about your exes, you're likely to get scratched off the list.

Thirty years ago I was working for IBM as a computer programmer. The project I worked on was fraught with problems. So I submitted an application for a position with a major computer software company. I got the interview, but after about 20 minutes I knew they would not hire me. I was extremely negative and I never heard from them again.

If you are angry, unhappy, and/or miserable you absolutely need to get past that. What you need to do is focus on what you want and where you want to go. Think of the light at the end of the tunnel.

Can you picture where you want to go? What does it look like?

Let's start by describing the boss you'd love to have.

I have many clients who want and very much need someone who is very collegial or almost a peer. I have other clients who very much want someone who is in control. What I find most common is the desire to have a boss who is politically astute and gives my client complete control to do what needs to get done.

> *It is my claim that when you can state clearly and succinctly what you want, you will have friends, colleagues and countrymen come to your aid.*

My favorite boss was Theresa who managed the IBM AIX Briefing Center in Austin. She was phenomenally good at hiring superstars and then leaving them alone to do their jobs. If anything went wrong or there was political conflict she was right there to back us up. She was not competent to make technical decisions and left those to her team.

Best manager I have ever had.

I have often talked to young engineers who assumed their bosses were better engineers than they were and teachers who assumed the principals must have been fantastic in the classroom. Neither of those is true. The skill set needed for your job may not mirror the sets needed for a manager, at all.

Who has been your best boss and what made them so good?

You need to craft the equivalent of an elevator pitch to say "This is what I am looking for." You need to be able to clearly and succinctly express what you want.

What size organization suits you best? What kind of environment is the best soil for you to work in? What kind of culture and organizational structure do you want? Create an elevator speech that defines all of that:

I am looking for a smaller organization in the xxx industry, where I get to lead a cohesive team developing yyy. I want a manager who will support me but allow me to run the show as I see fit...I want to work in an organization that values teamwork with minimal politics...

How long will this take to develop and perfect?

Probably longer than you think.

You will need to practice this on friends, significant others and anyone else that will provide constructive criticism.

Once you have crafted your "Here is what I want" pitch, you need to get out and talk to people. It is my claim that when you can state clearly and succinctly what you want, you will have friends, colleagues and countrymen come to your aid. The key point is clarity and succinctness!

This is a real key to future happiness: Know what you want, and know how to ask for it.

ACTION STEPS

- ✓ Shift your thinking about job seeking to a dating mindset. You won't just take whoever will have you, you're looking for a good fit, too.

- ✓ Craft a pitch succinctly stating exactly what you want: "I want an executive position with a lot of autonomy in a small, but thriving, HR firm."

- ✓ Share your pitch with everyone you meet.

VETTING THE COMPANY

I have a client who told me that she had interviewed with one of the very sexy startups in town about six months earlier. She got to the finals and lost. So I asked why she wanted to work at a startup. The fact is this startup had a horrid reputation for hiring people and quickly chewing them up. My client acknowledged that the candidate who was hired was fired six weeks later. When they approached my client about the position after the firing, my client said "No thanks!"

Before approaching a company about a job, you should do your due diligence:

- Research the company on sites like Glassdoor.com

- Connect with recruiters or HR professionals at the target company on Linked In. This will give you visibility to the organization needed.

- Target former employees who have personal relationships with people you know. I would ask each of my connections to see if they have a personal relationship with the target employee and would be comfortable giving a personal introduction.

- Find out what these current and former employees think of the hiring manager. If they are current employees and they work for the hiring manager, be aware they might not be truthful... or they may be evasive. Be aware of their body language. Former employees will likely be more forthcoming with the truth.

Check Linked In for recommendations.

Go to the hiring manager's profile and check their recommendations section:

- Have they given recommendations to their employees?

- Have their employees recommended their manager?

Check other profiles within the organization to determine if there is a culture of giving recommendations on Linked In. If that is not in the company's culture it's a bad sign. You find this culture more commonly, by the way, in newer and smaller organizations than in big multinational companies.

PREPARE FOR THE INTERVIEW

The interview is like the first date. And on the first date, it's not all about whether the other person likes you...it's your date, too. What do you like or not like about the company? Are you ready with your elevator speech about what you need?

This interview is your interview. It is about whether you want the job. I was talking to a small business owner yesterday and she told me that she always starts the interview with "Do you have any questions about the position?" If the interviewee says no, then the interview is pretty much over. She wants to hire people who are looking for her company, not just "A Job."

You should come into any interview with at least 10 questions that you would like to have answered. Print them out and keep them in front of you. Take notes and record the interviewer's answers on the paper. Writing down the responses gives you time to think about where to take the conversation next!

Controlled pauses (that is my term) give you a chance to think about the flow of the conversation. Another example of a controlled pause is to restate the question you were just asked. "Let me make sure I understand your question. You asked...."

Pay attention to your gut instincts. If it does not feel right, it is probably not a good fit.

Remember it is your interview! Among your questions should be:

- What is the management style of the hiring manager?
- What is the team environment like?
- What is the reward structure?

- How structured is the work environment?
- How much freedom is allowed in the job to do it the way you want to do it?

You will likely interview with peers of the hiring manager, upper level managers and peers of the position you are pursuing. Use the first two questions with each. Beware that your future peers may be deceptive. Also, look for very different answers coming from different levels of management. My last manager was amazing at managing up and lousy at managing down. His management team had a very different opinion of him than the people he managed. Look for discrepancies.

When you interview with the hiring manager ask the following:

- Describe your management style.
- Give me three words that describe you at work.
- What do you like best about being a manager?

Most hiring managers are not very good at interviewing. Most have never been trained on interviewing skills. When you take this approach they often like it. If the hiring manager balks at any of these you might want to dig deeper.

Sometimes you will have to dig and read body language to get an accurate gauge on the situation. Given the information you have received from current and former employees, you should be able to play detective.

Pay attention to your gut instincts. If it does not feel right, it is probably not a good fit.

Have you not followed your instincts and regretted it? It all comes down to you taking responsibility for the process.

ACTION STEPS

✓ Check out the company before the interview. Look on sites like Glassdoor.com and talk to people who work for the company and former employees to learn about the culture.

✓ Look at the company's Linked In site to see if it receives and gives recommendations. This could be a sign of the company's level of supportiveness.

✓ Prepare a list of at least 10 questions you want answered before you decide to take the job.

THE DREADED QUESTION

It is all but guaranteed that somewhere in the interview process you will be asked the following question:

"Why do you want to leave your current position?"

Whatever answer you prepare for this, also prepare for the fact that the interviewer may keep harping on it in one form or another to see if you will start spilling angry beans. Have a strategy against taking the bait. Our goal is to have a response that pivots the response from what you are leaving — to – where you are going! It is all about re-framing the question. You might respond *– I am happy in my current position (whether this is true or not) but I am looking for — what this new job can actually provide.*

WHEN YOU NEED MORE LOVE AND MORE MONEY

Let's use Robert as an example.

He's a political science lecturer at a major university in the Midwest.

He had been an energy lobbyist until the 9/11 disaster and the Enron bankruptcy put him out of work.

He went back to school to get his master's degree in political science and landed a lecturer position at the university he had attended.

His pay is very low, he has been teaching the same classes for many years, and his ego has taken a bruising.

He is the kind of guy who really likes the pat on the back from his bosses, which he does not receive. He gets appreciation from his students, but not from anyone else at the school.

The tedium of teaching the same classes has gotten to him. He has realized he needs a lot of variety to keep him motivated.

He needs to make more money. He is married with two kids and the money is not sufficient. He is not on a tenure track and therefore, it is somewhat of a dead end job.

He wants a position as an energy lobbyist.

> *Do not get negative! If you find anything you say sounds, smells, or tastes negative — stop — regroup — start again with a positive tone.*

How could Robert respond when posed with the magic question on why he is leaving?

One possible response could be:

I love my job and my students but what I really want is a position where I can get some recognition for my work, where I get to work on a wide variety of topics and I can make enough money to support my family.

If the interviewer comes back and asks — Do you not get that from your current position?

Robert could respond:

My salary is of public record and you can look that up. I am focused on where I want to go and your position seems to meet my criteria. Can I ask you about the variety of topics I would be working on at this position?

He can pivot the response to where he was going and, when questioned, use it as a way to pose a question back to the interviewer.

Robert was focused on what he wanted and was not going to take the bait!

Practice this yourself. Can you be prepared to pivot back with a question?

WHEN YOU NEED MORE STATUS AND MORE FREEDOM

Let's talk about James this time.
He works for a huge insurance company as director of HR, responsible for managing the medical benefits.

He has been climbing the corporate ladder with a plan to be a VP.

He is not happy in his current position working for a huge slow moving organization.

He has worked for medium size companies where he has had a leadership role in HR.

His boss Steve, VP of HR, who he just adored, left because Steve's boss was a workaholic and expected all of his staff to do the same.

After much thought, James has decided he would rather work for a smaller company again. He wants to be a big fish in small pond.

He has applied and is interviewing for Steve's old VP position but cannot see himself working for the workaholic boss. If offered the job, he will be put in a very difficult position because he has a family and wants a personal life.

He is interviewing for the Director of HR for a small/medium size company that is growing rapidly. He would have a small staff but would be responsible for the HR for the entire company.

How should James answer the question — Why do you want to leave your current position?

One response could be:

I want to work for a smaller company where I can have an impact on all phases of HR within the company. I want to work in a dynamic environment. Can we talk about the new initiatives that are planned for the coming year?

James did not answer the question but stated where he wanted to go which implied why he might be leaving.

He immediately pivoted the conversation to a topic he wanted to discuss. Whenever you are posed with a question that has bait attached, deflect the bait and pivot the conversation back the other way.

WHEN YOU NEED TO BE IN CHARGE OF THE PROCESS

For the third, and last, scenario we have Mary.

Mary works for a very large technology company in marketing operations. She is very good at her job.

She likes to be able to control her schedule. Her current job is completely interrupt driven, which drives her nuts!

Mary needs to work in an environment where she knows who is in control. She has had a new manager every six months for the last three years. Not Good!

Mary has a very high social service interest; she likes to help people. She coaches girls' soccer teams and just loves it. She has networked her way into a smaller organization where she has applied for an HR position.

How should Mary answer the question — Why do you want to leave your current position?

One response could be:

I want to take my operations skills and transition them into a position where I can have an impact on people's lives. I want a stable work and management environment. How long have you been the manager of this team and how would you describe your management style.

She asked for what she wanted and immediately pivoted the conversation back to the interviewer.

What should you NOT do?

GET NEGATIVE! If you find anything you say sounds, smells, or tastes negative — stop — regroup — start again with a positive tone.

Mary should not say that she dislikes being interrupt driven or that she dislikes that her manager changes every six months. It is her responsibility to ask enough questions to find out whether the environment is to her liking.

I cannot state this enough – this is like dating and marriage! Both sides need to come prepared to find out whether this is a match.

ACTION STEPS

✓ Formulate a positive-sounding response to the question: Why do you want to leave your current position?

✓ Practice answering uncomfortable questions by asking the interviewer a question.

✓ Avoid anything that looks, smells or sounds even the least bit negative!

HOW TO NEGOTIATE TO GET WHAT YOU WANT

Before you can start negotiating, you have to know what you want. Most people think this is about money. I say bull hockey. Think for a moment, what have been the most critical things that have made you happy in your past jobs?

I will almost guarantee you that they were not monetary.

When I took my last corporate gig in December of 2007, my wife and I had planned a three week trip to Italy for September 2008. I was offered a position to build a sales training program and September is the third and last month of the quarter. This is usually when sales teams are going full blast to make their numbers. I made it very clear that my wife was the real boss. What I wanted was to have these three weeks be paid time off whether I had PTO time available or not. As it turns out, we did not go to Italy. The recession set in and we went to Oregon for two weeks.

My boss did not question me taking vacation during September.

INTANGIBLES ARE WORTH MORE THAN CASH

What is important to you?

- Work from home?
- Child care?
- Pet care or maybe you want to bring your dog to the office?
- Schedule? Maybe the traffic is horrible at certain times of day. You can negotiate the time you need to be in the office.
- Desk chair? After I ruptured the L4/L5 disc in my back, I learned how important a proper desk chair can be.
- Cell phone? For years, I refused to take a company phone. If it is my phone, I have the right not to answer it!

Develop a list of the items that are important to you. Remember the non-financial requirements are likely more important than the financial ones. Negotiate on the non-financial items first! Once they have made an offer, they have made a commitment to hiring you. They will not easily walk away. Use that to your advantage. It often turns out money is the least important negotiating point but is usually the one we put the most emphasis on!

FINANCIAL REQUIREMENTS

Never ever tell them what you currently make or what you want! Never! Never! Never! Know what you are worth! Talk to peers. The world has changed and people will talk about compensation. Look at the entire compensation including salary, benefits, 401(k) match, stock option, employee stock purchase plans, etc.

Check some of these websites for salary comparisons:

- Salary.com
- Glassdoor.com Salary Comparison
- Indeed.com Salary Search

When you are given an offer, never ever accept it on the same day. If they insist on an immediate answer, then walk away as fast as you can! The answer is no. If the offer is low, tell them you want more. If they ask how much more you want, you respond I want to be compensated fairly. Do not take the bait!

I am currently working with a client who expects an offer in the next week. He has been working for the same employer for over 30 years. I have him very focused on the work environment and following his gut instincts. He is currently working on the intangible/non-financial requirements so that he is prepared when the offer letter comes.

Never ever tell them what you currently make or what you want! Never! Never! Never! Know what you are worth!

This includes vacation with specific dates, office and home office requirements, his exact start date (he is relocating and wants to take a month off) and other non-financial requirements.

I will have him negotiate all of this including the exact dates for his vacation before he gets to the financial numbers.

So remember:

- Learn everything you can about the company and the hiring manager before even going after the job. It may not be worth your trouble to get dressed up for interview.

- Prepare 10 questions for the interview; make sure you're learning what you need to know about whether the company suits you.

- Be ready to answer the question: Why do you want to leave your current position without taking the bait to be negative.

- Have your list of non-financial needs ready and negotiate those first.

This is you, taking charge of your Career Pivot.

ACTION STEPS

- ✓ Make a list of all intangibles you want before you begin negotiating with the company. This might include anything from flex time to a good office chair.

- ✓ Never divulge what you earn or what you hope to make. Make the company give the offer.

- ✓ Never answer immediately.

TIME TO ROLL UP YOUR SLEEVES

Let's face it, it would be great if we could snap our fingers and Poof! We have a new career, a better body, a fatter retirement account or if we could undo some of our history. While you can't undo it, you can use what you've learned from it to make a better future.

From reviewing your past jobs, to looking at what makes you happy, to building a tribe, all these tasks take time. Whatever your personality, talents, or temperament, you're going to run into something along the way that really challenges you personally. For me, it was asking for help. For some people, it might be taking on social media, facing a truth in one's assessment, or just being on the bottom of the totem pole again. That's alright, being personally challenged can be a good thing.

Don't give up. As we've all acknowledged, retirement at 65 is no longer a reality for most people. You have decades ahead of you that are going to be spent working. Isn't it worthwhile to invest some time now to create work you can enjoy? I know I'll probably be working the rest of my life. But I'd like it to be doing something I like for fewer hours than I used to spend at the office.

Be methodical. You can't make all these changes at once. Start with understanding yourself, your history and your needs and work from there. If you want more help or guidance, I've also begun a series of webinars entitled Stop the Career Insanity—helping people to avoid falling into the same traps over and over again. I also take on individual clients with packages that range from short assessments of where they are to a long-term commitment to reach that final destination.

Make me part of your tribe!

Thanks for letting me share my journey with you and I wish you the best of everything in your search for a career that will grow with you!

ABOUT THE AUTHORS

Marc Miller's career journey included 22 years at IBM, several thriving tech startups, a painful stint as a high school teacher, a gig raising funds for the Jewish Community Association of Austin and a near fatal bicycle accident that changed his perspective forever.

Thirty years of wandering the proverbial career desert, often repeating the same mistakes over and over, taught him his most crucial lesson: Most people don't really know what makes them happy at their core, what fulfills them.

They pursue money, status, a skill set, all of which provide some level of satisfaction, but not contentment. They wind up feeling frustrated and trapped. Others have figured out what they need, but don't know how to chart a course to get there.

An active member of the Launch Pad Job Club, Marc found himself counseling friends and associates on their career journeys and finally realized he'd found his vocation. He would use his extensive training experience to help others—especially Baby Boomers—find careers that they could grow into for the decades that lie ahead.

Marc is passionate about his work and the clients he serves. He's taught in more than 35 countries and helped clients from many industries.

Susan Lahey has always been passionate about words—as a medium—and story. Especially true stories about ordinary people plucking up the courage to do something new and overcome obstacles, which describes Marc Miller and the clients he serves.

She grew up in the newsroom of *The Kansas City Star* and worked as a business reporter, then worked as associate editor of a business/lifestyle magazine. Her long freelance career has included writing about everything from art to banking to sustainable building techniques for national and regional publications. In Austin, she reports on startups and emerging technologies, non-profits and other topics in addition to running her own content marketing company: Fishpond Content.